CD INCLUDED

HAL•LEONARD
BIG BAND
PLAY-ALONG
VOLUME 3

Duke Ellington

TENOR SAX

ISBN: 978-1-4234-4977-5

HAL•LEONARD®
CORPORATION
7777 W. BLUEMOUND RD. P.O. BOX 13819 MILWAUKEE, WI 53213

Visit Hal Leonard Online at
www.halleonard.com

CD INCLUDED

HAL•LEONARD
BIG BAND
PLAY-ALONG
VOLUME 3

Duke Ellington

CARAVAN

Words and Music by DUKE ELLINGTON,
IRVING MILLS and JUAN TIZOL
Arranged by MICHAEL SWEENEY

TENOR SAX

TENOR SAX

CHELSEA BRIDGE

By BILLY STRAYHORN
Arranged by MARK TAYLOR

TENOR SAX

TENOR SAX

COTTON TAIL

TENOR SAX

By DUKE ELLINGTON
Arranged by MARK TAYLOR

TENOR SAX

Featured in SOPHISTICATED LADIES

I'M BEGINNING TO SEE THE LIGHT

Words and Music by DON GEORGE, JOHNNY HODGES,
DUKE ELLINGTON and HARRY JAMES

Arranged by MARK TAYLOR

TENOR SAX

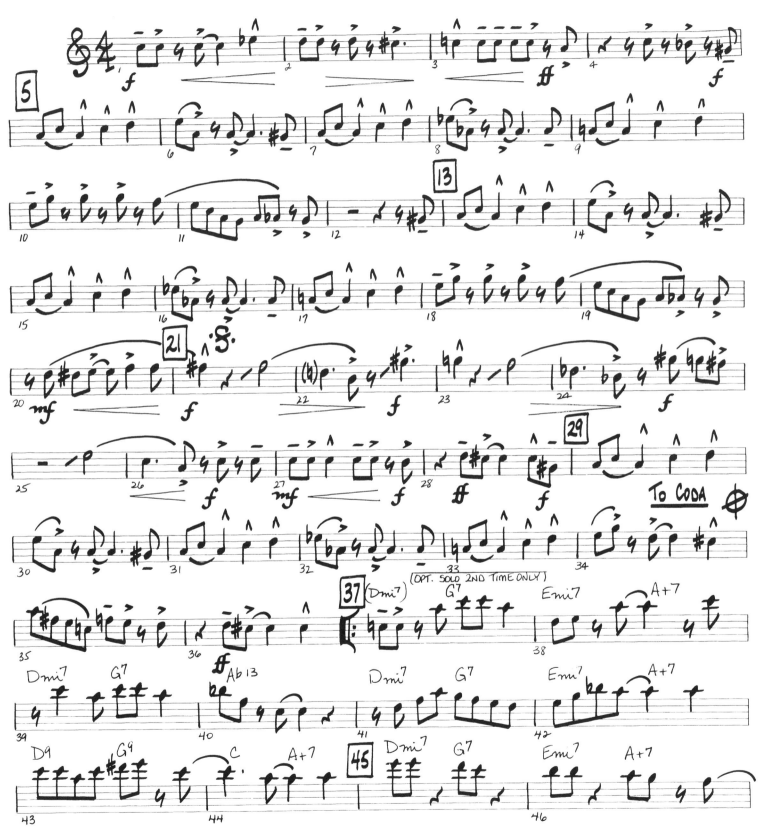

TENOR SAX

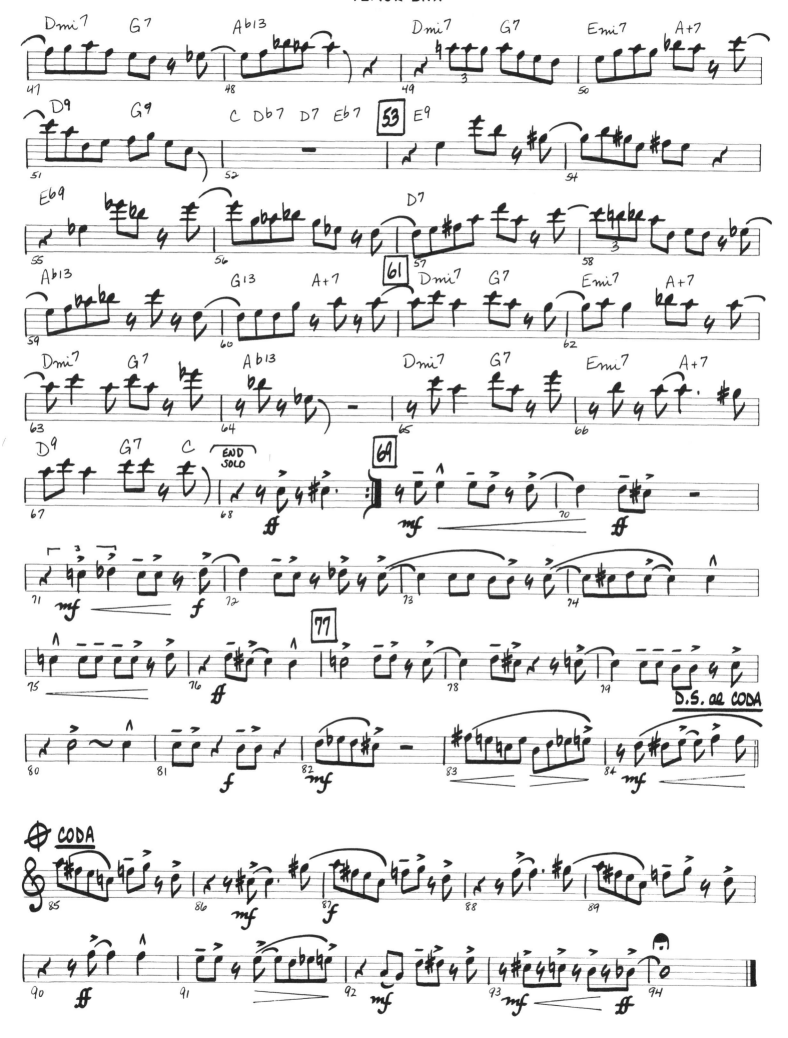

I'M JUST A LUCKY SO AND SO

Words by MACK DAVID
Music by DUKE ELLINGTON
Arranged by ROGER HOLMES

TENOR SAX

TENOR SAX

IN A MELLOW TONE

Tenor Sax

By Duke Ellington
Arranged by MARK TAYLOR

TENOR SAX

IN A SENTIMENTAL MOOD

By Duke Ellington
Arranged by MARK TAYLOR

TENOR SAX

TENOR SAX

Mood Indigo

Tenor Sax

Words and Music by DUKE ELLINGTON,
IRVING MILLS and ALBANY BIGARD
Arranged by JOHN BERRY

TENOR SAX

SATIN DOLL

TENOR SAX

By Duke Ellington
Arranged by MARK TAYLOR

TENOR SAX

TAKE THE "A" TRAIN

Words and Music by
BILLY STRAYHORN

Arranged by *DAVE BARDUHN*

TENOR SAX

TENOR SAX